OLD TELEVISION

Andrew Emmerson

Shire Publications

The Televisor of 1930 was the first television receiver produced in quantity. Its pictures, although small and of thirty lines definition, were of genuine entertainment quality and considered a marvel of their time. It was manufactured for the Baird company by Plessey Ltd, and the few surviving examples command high prices.

CONTENTS

Cover: *Demonstrating a brand-new television set in the mid 1950s. In those days televisions were proper pieces of furniture and destined to become the focal point of the living room. The pattern seen on the screen, known as Test Card C, was transmitted before the main pro- grammes started and was accompanied at most times by tuneful music. In this way viewers could check the picture and sound quality of their sets.*

ACKNOWLEDGEMENTS
Thanks are due to all who contributed help and information, and particularly to the following for the supply of photographs: the BBC, the BT Museum and Archives, Ray Herbert, Jonathan Hill, Dicky Howett, Jeremy Jago, Steve James, Bernard King, and Reed Business Publishing Ltd (publishers of *Television* magazine, successor to *Practical Television*).

British Library Cataloguing in Publication Data: Emmerson, Andrew. Old Television. – (Shire album; 337) 1. Television – Receivers and reception – History 2. Television broadcasting – History 3. Television broadcasting – Social aspects I. Title 384.5'5'09 ISBN 0 7478 0367 6.

Published in 1998 by Shire Publications Ltd, Cromwell House, Church Street, Princes Risborough, Buckinghamshire HP27 9AA, UK. Copyright © 1998 by Andrew Emmerson. First published 1998. Shire Album 337. ISBN 0 7478 0367 6.

Printed in Great Britain by CIT Printing Services, Press Buildings, Merlins Bridge, Haverfordwest, Pembrokeshire SA61 1XF.

The transmitting aerials at Alexandra Palace in north London are one of the most enduring images of early television. The strange spiky shape of the top of the tower became a symbol of television and was seen nightly in the opening sequence of 'Television Newsreel' for many years.

INTRODUCTION

This book is intended as a handy guide to television in general, and to viewing television in particular. It explores the history of a communications medium that is now almost universal but was originally out of reach of all but the well-off. It looks at how it began, how it developed and how it works.

Television is now more than seventy years old, and major anniversaries have already been passed in several countries. As a result, old television receivers, ephemera and even old television programmes are today attracting an unprecedented level of interest. This account puts into context what probably appears to some as a fascinating but strangely unfamiliar subject but to others represents the golden age of black and white television.

The period covered by this book ends immediately following the introduction of colour television to Britain in 1969. For some viewers that time is already the dim and distant past; for others their first television memories were of the Coronation broadcast of 1953 or even the pioneering programmes of the pre-war era. This book is for anyone who enjoys an interest in the television of the past.

THE EARLIEST DAYS OF TELEVISION

In this age of global satellite broadcasting and the imminent advent of digital pictures with high definition, television is an up-to-the-minute medium. The technology of television, on the other hand, already has a rich and colourful past.

Like sound radio, television cannot be claimed as the concept of a single inventor. Numerous experimenters contributed ideas and improvements to the technology of bringing moving pictures with sound into the home. What is indisputable is that the first person to exploit television commercially was the Scottish inventor John Logie Baird (1888-1946). Starting in 1925, he used an electromechanical system to scan images for transmission; a rotating disc, about 18 inches (46 cm) across and pierced with holes in a spiral, produced a picture made up of thirty 'slices' or lines (these were vertical, unlike the horizontal scanning system of today). Because of the persistence of human vision, viewers saw a complete picture, the viewing device being a neon lamp in front of which rotated another disc pierced with holes. By keeping the transmitting and receiving discs in synchronism, viewers could see over a radio link (or by closed circuit wires) an exact replica of the transmitted scene.

Although the pictures were flickering and no larger than a postcard, they were true moving pictures. From 1929 to 1935 television programmes were transmitted by the BBC on the Baird thirty-line system, and it would be wrong to belittle this achievement. Nonetheless, despite many improvements, the electromechanical system was inflexible and was no match for the more versatile electronic method of television that was to follow.

As events transpired, the techniques devised by John Logie Baird were to have next to nothing to do with the television system we watch today. A more significant turning point was the start in 1936 of regular transmissions of electronic television, devised by a team of engineers from EMI Ltd led by Isaac Shoenberg. In this kind of television the scanning is done electronically by deflecting a beam of electrons, both in the pick-up tube of the camera and within the cathode-ray tube

John Logie Baird is often called the 'father of television', although the electronic television systems of today have little to do with the electromechanical techniques he employed in the late 1920s and early 1930s. His most significant contribution was to develop public awareness of television. This superb quarter-scale model of a Baird Televisor set was made by Bernard King. Visible on the right is the viewing window, whilst the circular casing at the rear covered the scanning disc, which rotated at 750 revolutions per minute.

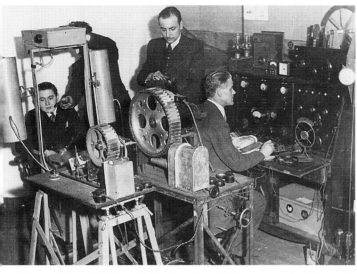

Television equipment of the electro-mechanical era tends to have a Heath-Robinson air, an impression which this photograph taken in 1934 confirms. In this experimental studio are mirror-drum transmitters for thirty- and sixty-line pictures. Note the reflectors for the many light bulbs needed to illuminate the subject being televised, and also the 'spinning disc' receiver on the shelf at upper right.

of the receiver. The image is built up line by line, transmitted over the airwaves one line at a time, and recreated on the viewing screen in the same way, fifty times a second.

The fundamental principles of television have not changed since 1936, and the only major differences have been improved picture definition (achieved by increasing the number of lines in the television picture) and the enhancement of colour. In Britain both of these changes were made in the 1960s: 625-line transmissions began in 1964, although the original 405-line signals continued until 1985. Colour, on the Phase Alternate Line (PAL) system, was introduced in 1969.

It is notable that the television heritage that this book celebrates is a genuine British achievement: the world's first electronic television transmissions came from London, using an all-British system devised by engineers from the EMI and Marconi companies; the BBC had the distinction of providing the world's first regular service of entertainment programmes in high-definition, as the 405-line service was called in those days; the studios and transmitters at Alexandra Palace in north London were pioneer installations and set the pace for television development throughout the world in the years to come. Other countries soon followed suit – France in 1937, Germany in 1938 and the USA in 1939 – while just before the Second World War experimental services were starting

'Oh, you're wasting your time with wireless – the thing now is television!' Television was a ready inspiration for humour in the 1930s.

Vol. 3. No. 67. Week ending August 27, 1938

TWOPENCE
EVERY WEDNESDAY

LIGHTING SQUAD

LIGHTING SQUAD

6 STAGE HANDS
& PROPERTY MEN

"SET" FOR
VARIETY
PROGRAMME

CABLES FROM
CAMERAS TO
"O.B" VAN

2 CAMERA MEN

4 MAKE-UP
ASSISTANTS

2ND CAMERA

BOOM
"MIKE"
(1 MAN)

"PROP"
MEN

ANNOUNCER

STAGE
MANAGER

CABLES FROM
CAMERAS

"SET" FOR
PERSONAL TELEVISION
OF VISITORS

LIGHTING
SQUAD

TELEVISION
AT RADIOLYMPIA

A BIRD'S-EYE view of the television studio that the B.B.C. have built at Radiolympia for this year's radio exhibition.

Programmes will be radiated from this studio to receivers all over the exhibition where many thousands of visitors will have the good fortune to witness television in progress, many of them doubtless for the first time.

Round the walls of the studio are the lighting men concentrating their spotlights on the set on which televising is already in progress. There are three television cameras in the studio. On the left-hand side are the property men and scene shifters busily building another set from which the next scene will be shot. In the centre foreground is the position from which specially invited visitors will be televised, and just to the right of the first camera is the sound department.

All the way round the studio are long windows through which visitors will be able to watch the whole process of television. This is probably the first time television has been demonstrated to the public on such a large scale.

Television was always the main attraction for the public at pre-war Radiolympia home entertainment exhibitions in London. The BBC relayed outside broadcasts from this ocean-liner set constructed at the show, a major technical achievement in 1938.

in Japan, Russia and some other European countries. But it was in Britain where television made the most impact and where between 1936 and 1939 television programming, entertainment and technology were developed to a remarkable state of completeness.

Although television was seen as a wonder of the age, its social impact was slight in

The high cost of sets was one of the reasons why television was not a mass entertainment medium before the Second World War. This Marconiphone 707 combined radio and television receiver was one of the cheaper sets, costing around six weeks' earnings. Very attractively designed and highly sought after today by collectors, it was made in 5 inch (13 cm) and 7 inch (18 cm) screen versions, which meant that the picture was only just watchable.

the years from 1936 to 1939. It was a rich person's pleasure, with the least expensive sets costing around £30, six times the average weekly wage. Although some twenty thousand sets were sold, nearly all in the London area, television for most people was a novelty no more affordable than, for example, a helicopter would be today. Soon the Second World War brought a reappraisal of broadcasting priorities, and all thoughts of television were forgotten for seven years.

That is not to say that television had no role to play during the war. Radar equipment borrowed heavily from television circuitry and the production facilities built up before the war for television. The design of the main Chain Home radar

transmitters was based on a Baird television transmitter, whilst an off-the-shelf Pye receiver component design was used in many radar receivers. Even the BBC's television transmitter at Alexandra Palace was pressed into service for 'bending the beams' of hostile radar signals and confusing the enemy.

For those to whom money was no object, this HMV model 703 'Mastergram' of 1937 combined television, radio and an auto-gramophone and was launched for the Coronation of King George VI. It is said that only eight were sold.

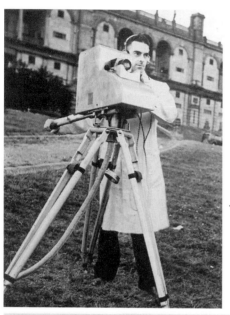

Inevitably the very first television programmes were studio-bound but it did not take the engineers long before they ventured outdoors. The station's engineer-in-charge, Douglas Birkinshaw, operates an Emitron camera on the slopes below the Alexandra Palace studios and transmitter site.

Below: *Televising the Derby from Epsom was rightly considered a wonder of the age before the Second World War. Until then the only live coverage had been by sound radio, with pictures following in the next day's newspaper or a day or two later in cinema newsreels. Television brought home the event in sight and sound. All the key elements of pre-war television are seen in this drawing: the Emitron camera, the mirror-lid TV receiver, the mobile scanner van and the Alexandra Palace aerials.*

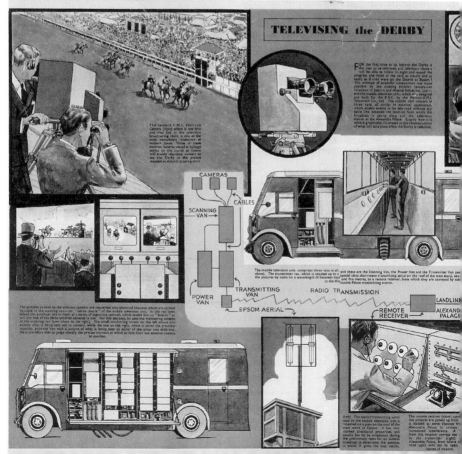

TELEVISING the DERBY

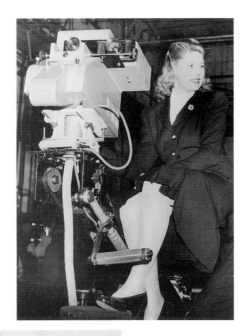

Television Programmes

An hour's special film transmission intended for the industry only will be given from 11 a.m. to 12 noon each weekday, except Tuesday.

Sound	Vision
41.5 Mc/s.	45 Mc/s.

THURSDAY, MAY 19th.

3, Demonstration of National Dances of Hungary, Poland and Russia. **3.20,** Gaumont-British News. **3.30,** 147th edition of Picture Page.

8.15 (sound only), London Music Festival at Queen's Hall: Toscanini conducting the B.B.C. Symphony Orchestra. **9.5,** Cabaret. **9.30,** British Movietonews. **9.40,** 148th edition of Picture Page. **10,** News Bulletin.

FRIDAY, MAY 20th.

3-4, "Viceroy Sarah," the play by Norman Ginsbury, with Marie Ney in the name part.

9, Starlight. **9.10,** Gaumont-British News. **9.20,** "Charles and Mary"—excerpts from the play by Joan Temple. Cast includes Peter Ridgeway, Joan Temple and Patricia Hayes. **10.30,** News Bulletin.

SATURDAY, MAY 21st.

3, Jack Hylton and his Band. **3.35,** Gaumont-British News. **3.45,** In Our Garden, C. H. Middleton.

9, "Sweet and Hot," a little show with Eric Wild and his Band. **9.30,** British Movietonews. **9.40,** "They're Off"—a melodrama of the Turf. Cast includes Queenie Leonard, Eric Fawcett and Charles Wade. **10.15,** News Bulletin.

SUNDAY, MAY 22nd.

3-3.30, O.B. from Chelsea Flower Show. Mr. C. H. Middleton, Mr. Freddie Grisewood and Miss Elizabeth Cowell will accompany the cameras during this and the remaining two transmissions.

8.50, News Bulletin. **9.5,** Egon Petri, pianoforte. **9.15,** Film. **9.25-10.30,** "Pride and Prejudice," an adaptation of Jane Austen's famous novel.

MONDAY, MAY 23rd.

3, "Broadway"—one of the first American gangster stories. The play was written by Philip Dunning and George Abbott. **4.15-4.30,** O.B. from Chelsea Flower Show.

8.15 (sound only), Relay from Queen's Hall of part of the Symphony Concert, conducted by Toscanini. **9.5,** Cabaret. **9.40,** British Movietonews. **9.50,** Flower Decoration—talk by Constance Spry. **10.5,** Music Makers: Jean Norris. **10.15,** News Bulletin.

TUESDAY, MAY 24th.

11-11.30 a.m., O.B. from Chelsea Flower Show. **3,** Intimate Cabaret. **3.20,** British Movietonews. **3.30,** The Ballets Joose in "Seven Heroes."

9, Speaking Personally. **9.10,** Yvette Guildert, the French actress. **9.25,** Catch-as-Catch-Can Wrestling. **9.40,** Gaumont-British News. **9.50,** Starlight. **10,** News Bulletin.

WEDNESDAY, MAY 25th.

3, Forecast of Fashion. **3.15,** Gaumont-British News. **3.25,** "They're Off," as on Saturday at 9.40 p.m.

9, As at 3 p.m. **9.15,** An account of his search for rare birds in Greenland, by Reynold Bray. **9.30,** British Movietonews. **9.40,** "The Wife of Bath's Tale," a Pepler masque. **10.10,** News Bulletin.

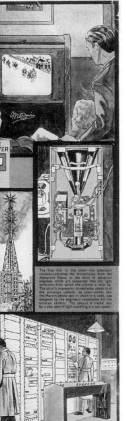

Above: *Television made household names (and faces) of its many personalities. One of the most familiar to early viewers was Jasmine Bligh, who introduced television programmes before the war and for a while afterwards. Here she takes the cameraman's viewpoint on one of the Emitron cameras used in those days*

Right: *The television schedule in this typical week of May 1938 provided spartan fare, but viewers then were doubtless grateful for programmes of any kind.*

THE POST-WAR ERA

The growing prosperity of the 1950s and 1960s made them the period in which television entered the lives of nearly everyone. Television was probably the most powerful influence on the people who grew up in these decades, whilst for the people who made the programmes (and the sets) this black and white era was a golden age of opportunity, creativity and progress. This was also the era when television first created a broad popular culture of its own. Television became a topic of universal discussion, and its images were instantly recognisable: H-shaped aerials appeared on roof tops everywhere, and even the little green men from outer space portrayed in newspaper cartoons had an obligatory 'H' antenna grafted on their heads. Television had arrived.

Two factors were responsible for this: rising prosperity, and the Coronation of Queen Elizabeth II. As earnings rose in real terms in the early 1950s, a growing number of people could afford television, especially in the Midlands, where the motor industry and other manufacturing trades were providing good employment, and where Britain's second television transmitter had been opened in 1949. Many people took only modest holidays and did not own cars, so television now represented a kind of entertainment and escapism they could afford. To make it easier, firms made it possible to rent a set or buy one

An actual off-screen photograph from the broadcast of the Coronation of Queen Elizabeth II in 1953. This event, more than any other, brought television into the public consciousness. Many people bought a set specifically to watch the spectacle; those who could not afford to were invited to watch with neighbours.

In 1955 independent television began broadcasting in Britain. At last viewers had a choice of programme, and for the first few months they virtually deserted the BBC.

on hire purchase. Gifted individuals built their own receivers from war-surplus radar components.

The televising of the Coronation in 1953 stimulated the sale of sets in two ways. It finally settled the decision many people had been postponing for so long, and those who had to watch the ceremony on their neighbours' set decided afterwards it was time they had a set as well. Two years later, the coming of a second channel, ITV, with its more down-to-earth offering, started a trend for brighter, more popular programmes that was reflected on the BBC as well.

Not everyone was television-minded, though, and for some households the wireless remained the sole source of broadcast entertainment. A few folk had difficulty in

Many people's fondest memories of old television are of the programmes of their childhood, such as 'Blue Peter'. This photograph showing presenter Valerie Singleton was taken in April 1965 at the the BBC Television Centre. Note the paraphernalia of cameras, cables, lights, cameramen and floor managers

Regional studios such as BBC Bristol had simpler technical requirements, and almost all that was needed was a camera, a picture monitor, a caption stand and a newsreader (Wynroe Thomas in this case). Note the characteristic four lenses on the camera: these were mounted on a rotary turret, and the cameraman chose a focal length appropriate to the shot. Zoom lenses did not become commonplace until the 1970s.

coming to terms with television altogether. Back in 1935 the Postmaster General had felt obliged to reassure listeners to BBC radio that television would not be a two-way process and that the set in the living room could not peer into their homes, and this idea that television could watch the viewers as they watched it took some time to die out. Even after the war, a woman in Wakefield whose habit was to take her bath in front of the fire did so with towels draped around her so that her idol, the television presenter Macdonald Hobley, could not 'see' her!

Right: *Some subtle psychology is employed in this poster of the early 1950s to ensure that exultant viewers took out a television licence.*

Below: *The demand for more exciting television in the 1950s and 1960s led to the expansion of outside broadcasts from events around Britain. Reflecting this trend were these Dinky Supertoy models for fortunate children. These toys were expensive when new (they were introduced in 1959) and now fetch three-figure sums if well preserved and in their original boxes. (Left) BBC mobile control room; (centre) extending mast microwave link vehicle; (right) Roving Eye camera vehicle.*

Please Remember

TO BUY YOUR £2 TELEVISION LICENCE AS SOON AS YOUR SET IS INSTALLED. AND CLAIM THE *REBATE* DUE TO YOU ON YOUR UNEXPIRED £1 LICENCE WHICH IS FOR SOUND ONLY

OBTAINABLE AT YOUR GPO LOCAL POST OFFICE

TELEVISION SETS OF THE 1950s AND 1960s

When television transmissions started in 1936, the sets on sale had a very different appearance from those of today. Because the picture tubes were very long, they were mounted vertically in a cabinet the size of a chest freezer, using a mirror angled at 45 degrees for viewing. These 'mirror-lid' sets, as they are called, were soon supplanted by direct-viewing sets with a horizontal picture tube, viewed in the 'normal' way, and after the Second World War only one mirror-lid set was produced. Viewers found console (floor-standing) or table sets much more convenient.

Until the mid 1950s large picture tubes were difficult to make, and the only large-screen sets made used a special optical arrangement to project their image on to a linen screen. This produced large pictures, some measuring as much as 4 feet by 3 feet (122 by 91 cm), although these were neither bright nor sharp by today's standards. Further disadvantages were the substantial size and weight of these models, comparable to a chest of drawers, and their price – between £120 and £360 at a time when conventional 12 inch (30 cm) sets cost around £70 or £80.

Most homes therefore made do with small screens – 9 inch (23 cm) and 12 inch (30 cm) tubes were commonplace – so that everyone had to crowd around to get a good view. An assortment of magnifying lenses – large, bulbous, made of Perspex and filled with paraffin that was originally clear but gradually became yellower – were supposed to make the picture look bigger but had little effect.

Magnifying lenses were also required for the home-built sets made in large numbers at this

Above: The largest screen size before the war was 12 inches (30 cm), as seen on this Bush model T18 of 1938. Sets were expensive and normally contained a good all-wave radio to help justify the high cost.

Right: After the war a number of manufacturers produced some extremely opulent sets, even though few customers could afford them. This is a McMichael model DL1 combined television and radiogram of 1948.

A display of pre-war television sets by Marconiphone and His Master's Voice, all finished in rich glossy veneers. The table sets seen in the centre offered a choice of 5 inch (13 cm) or 7 inch (18 cm) round screen and were suitable for smaller rooms. The 9 inch (23 cm) console and mirror-lid sets on either side were intended for more luxurious homes and needed several people to shift them into place.

Much more affordable was this Bush TV12, turned out with a 9 inch (23 cm) screen and a lustrous brown bakelite cabinet. Together with the follow-up model TV22, which looked very similar and cost just over £50, this was one of the most successful – and reliable – sets made in the post-war period. Many of these sets are still working today, and they are now highly prized by collectors.

time by enthusiastic amateurs. War-surplus radar parts were available cheaply, and magazines published blueprints and instructions to turn these into low-cost television receivers. Dealers sold kits of all the necessary parts, along with simple plywood cabinets. The chief disadvantages were the green screen of the radar tube and its small size; while magnifying lenses could enlarge the image, they could do nothing about the strange hue of the pictures.

What characterised most television receivers made until around 1960 was the quality of their cabinets, styled to match contemporary living-room furniture. Most sets had cabinets clad in high-quality wood veneers, and some even had tambour or cupboard doors to make them look more like a piece of furniture than a television receiver. Generally the wood was given a high-gloss cellulose finish, often tricked out with 'gold' aluminium trim and ivory plastic knobs with gold inlays. As furniture fashions changed towards more natural-looking veneers, so did television cabinets, and by the mid 1960s some very attractive teak and other veneers were being used. At the end

Some early post-war receivers must have looked hideous, even to the keenest buyer. This Pye model T102 table set, with 9 inch (23 cm) screen, dates from 1947 and has a veneered plywood cabinet, bakelite bezel around the screen and an expanded metal loudspeaker grille – not Pye's finest effort! Sets such as this cost around £50, at a time when the average weekly wage was no more than £6.

Left: This was an extremely successful and popular set in the mid 1950s. Also made by Pye of Cambridge (model VT4), it is popularly known as the 'Washboard' set on account of the ribbed wooden panel below the screen. (Washboards were an essential instrument of the musical 'skiffle' groups popular in those days.) It featured Automatic Picture Control and a tinted, tilted screen-guard to minimise room light reflections. This was important when television screens were less brilliant than today.

Below: Introduced in the 1960s, transistorised sets with lightweight plastic cabinets transformed the way people watched television. On the left is the Philips T-Vette (also sold as the Pye Gypsy), and next to it the late model Perdio Portarama. Both sets were dual-standard, meaning they could receive both 405-line VHF and 625-line UHF transmissions.

of this period some makers adopted the pop look by lacquering sets in white and other bold primary colours, but these were a little too stark for most households.

For cheaper receivers, alternative, less expensive materials had to be found. Some manufacturers, such as Bush and GEC, favoured cases made of polished brown bakelite, a tough but rather brittle plastic material, and these are firm favourites with collectors today, even though they were considered a cheap option in their day. Plywood covered with Rexene (a kind of imitation leathercloth) was chosen for the Ekco TMB270, the first portable combined television and radio set (ideal for picnics), and other manufacturers produced both wood and metal cases covered with the same material.

Later, small sets had cabinets made of plastics such as styrene and polypropylene; these were used on the British-made Perdio Portarama and the imported Japanese Sony TV9-306, both pioneering small-screen transistor portable sets. However, full-size sets continued to be made of wood.

Improved technology enabled larger screen sizes to be offered in the early 1950s, and most of these were used in floor-standing or 'console' receivers. This set, identified as an Ultra W721, was sold in Coronation year, 1953, and sports an occasional lamp in the 'Sputnik' style that was to become fashionable four or five years later. On many sets of this age the picture tube is all but exhausted, producing pictures that are barely visible. This problem can be overcome by having the tubes re-gunned or 'boosted'. Alternatively, it is still sometimes possible to find original replacement tubes.

15

Left: *The 1960s and 1970s were the era of the dual-standard receiver, which performed the tricky task of receiving two entirely different television systems: VHF transmissions on 405 lines and new 625-line pictures on UHF. This specimen is an Ultra 6638, adorned by various 1960s oddments. There is a marvellous orange Rotoflex 'rocket lamp' on the left, whilst on the set itself are a Dansette radio, a tasteful illuminated 'fish scene', a wobbly blue glass ashtray, and one of those bobbly ornaments that no one knows the name of. This set is a full-size 25 inch (64 cm) screen specimen, mounted on elegant legs.*

Right: *The Bush TV85, a 17 inch (43 cm) table model for BBC and ITV, typifies late 1950s set design. The Belling-Lee 'Golden V' set-top aerial is often called a 'rabbit's ears' antenna.*

The introduction of 625-line transmissions in 1964 brought a new technical complication to television receivers – the dual-standard set. Because the 405- and 625-line systems were so different technically, these new sets amounted to two separate receivers in one cabinet, sharing the same screen and loudspeaker. New sets had to incorporate both systems since it was known that broadcasts on the old 405-line system would be phased out eventually (although this did not happen until 1985). The launch of colour programmes across all channels in 1969 brought another refinement and some highly involved technology to produce colour pictures. These early colour sets were extremely expensive, very heavy and bulky and employed what was then leading-edge technology. Initially few were sold, and most had a fairly short life, being scrapped when more compact (and reliable) colour sets became available. For this reason early colour sets are somewhat rare, although not particularly valuable or collectable. Nearly all the sets made until the late 1960s used valves. Fundamentally different from the solid-state electronics of today, valves were much bulkier (making

Left: *The space age arrived in 1960 when Sony introduced the world's first all-transistor television. Everything about the set was different: its finish was two-tone grey wrinkle-painted steel, with stainless steel trim, whilst the adjustable sun visor and clever pull-out-and-twist rod antenna displayed thoughtful industrial design. As befits a design classic, this set can be seen in the Design Museum, London. This model, the TV8-301, was sold in Japan and North America but not in Britain. Sony's first British portable, the TV9-306, followed shortly after but looked far more conventional, with a rather unattractive shiny grey plastic finish.*

The Ultra Cub (also sold under the Ferguson and HMV names) is a typical mid 1960s British-made portable. Released in 1966, it was not light, weighing 15 pounds (6.8 kg), and cost 39 ½ guineas (£41 9s 6d). On the tuner BBC and ITV channels are paired next to one another (1 with 9, 2 with 10, 4 with 8 and so on) to minimise rotary movement when 'turning over' from BBC to ITV.

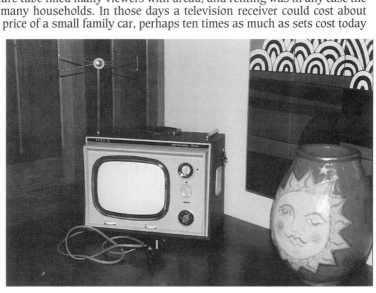

sets larger) and generated considerable heat (a source of unreliability). Over time this heat affected other components inside the set, causing control settings to drift. One of the reasons why the television companies broadcast a 'tuning signal' pattern before the start of the afternoon and evening programmes was that some owners needed time to 'tune in' their sets for the best possible picture. This instability also meant that many sets had more controls on the front panel, and some viewers enjoyed fiddling with these until they had what they thought was the perfect picture.

The valves also took several minutes to 'warm up'. Older viewers will remember the smell of burning dust coming from inside the set. Some manufacturers dared to turn this shortcoming into an asset, as in this extract from a Pye booklet of around 1949: 'Pye sets take about 2 minutes to warm up after they are switched on. This is because of the very complicated circuits which ensure picture stability. By allowing a longer warming up period, a much greater degree of final stability is achieved.'

Sets were also far less reliable than today, and the numerous breakdowns meant that the repair man was a frequent visitor to some households. Such was the unreliability and general uncertainty about the future of television (independent television and colour programmes were always rumoured to be 'just around the corner') that many people took the safer option of renting, rather than buying, their set. The high cost of a replacement picture tube filled many viewers with dread, and renting was in any case the only option for many households. In those days a television receiver could cost about one-sixth of the price of a small family car, perhaps ten times as much as sets cost today in real terms.

The Perdio Portarama 3, a British-made transistor portable for VHF (405-line) and UHF (625-line) viewing, is now rather hard to find. Note the bow-tie aerial for UHF.

THE CULTURE OF THE FIRST TELEVISION GENERATION

Periodic repeats of television programmes from days gone by provide us with an insight into the character of past programmes but not of the way in which they were seen at the time.

In most households in the 1950s viewing was a shared experience and something of a social event, just as sitting in a circle and listening to the 'wireless' had been before the Second World War. Viewers tended to accord more attention to programmes than they do today, when some people use television as little more than a background distraction. Receivers were neither portable nor cheap, so any home which had a television set made it the focus of the living room. This effect was emphasised by subdued room lighting, since screens were dimmer than today. It was considered bad for the eyes to watch television in total darkness, so 'tasteful' TV lights were sold to provide background illumination. Another essential was a television trolley or table, the latter in the obligatory contemporary style of rich glossy brown wood with tapering splayed legs in black, capped with lacquered brass ferrules.

Optional accessories were decorated leather covers for copies of the *Radio Times* and *TV Times* and stick-on screens that gave a 'lifelike' colour impression to television programmes ('winner of the Brussels Inventors Fair'). Some people were so desperate to have colour television, at a time when it was still no more than a laboratory novelty in Britain, that they bought these garish objects of translucent multi-coloured plastic

The small and rather dim screens of the 1950s gave rise to a lively trade in dubious add-ons claimed to enhance the pleasure of viewing. The polarised anti-glare filter ('It's dioptric, it's dependable') was supposed to improve picture contrast (not unlike computer monitor filters today), whilst the colour screen ('It enhances your television viewing') turned a black and white set into a colour one! The clear plastic overlay was tinted blue at the top (for sky), pink in the middle (for flesh tones) and green at the bottom (for grass). Amazingly, some people actually bought these accessories.

For some reason people felt it rather vulgar to leave on view periodicals such as the 'Radio Times' or 'TV Times'. Instead, they demonstrated their good taste with binders showing charming floral designs or even, in better-class homes, folders made of tooled leather.

to give their monochrome screens a 'coloured' effect!

Viewing hours were short until the early 1960s: perhaps a couple of hours around lunchtime, an hour's children's television from five o'clock until six, followed by the 'toddlers' truce' while small children were supposed to have their tea and then go to bed; the BBC news at 7 o'clock began another three hours' broadcasting and that was all. The introduction in 1955 of a second channel, ITV, brought in an element of keen competition, which enlivened programming and presentation on both channels.

Programmes were introduced by in-vision announcers, and the presentation of captions, weather maps and other ancillary items was less polished than the sophistication we expect today. Timekeeping on the BBC in particular was more an art than a science: with most programmes going out live, it was inevitable that sometimes they would overrun, or else finish early. Accordingly, a number of filler items were used when the next programme was not ready to start. People almost looked forward to

At the 'On The Air' Broadcasting Museum in Chester it is always time for tea! Afterwards, perhaps we shall watch Children's Television; we can look in the 'Radio Times' to see who is on today.

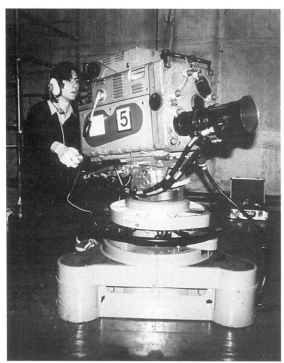

interlude films of spinning wheels, tropical fish, crashing waves or playful kittens, whilst the trick photography of the train that raced from London to Brighton in just four minutes was another favourite.

Less welcome were the dreaded captions 'Normal service will be resumed as soon as possible' and 'Do not adjust your set'. The first usually signified that the scheduled programme would be cancelled, since studio breakdowns were not uncommon. The second, no more than a catch-phrase today but used in earnest during the days of VHF broadcasting, heralded the foreign interference that could all but wipe out viewing. The VHF frequencies used were extremely prone to interference from foreign stations when abnormal atmospheric conditions caused transmissions to cover a wider area than usual. Severe patterning on pictures and foreign voices on the sound could reduce viewing enjoyment to zero in the summer months.

Electrical interference was also more pronounced, simply because fewer appliances were fitted with suppressors in

Above: *In the 1960s shooting television pictures was an energetic job. The cameras and supports were extremely large and cumbersome, yet cameramen managed to manoeuvre them with poise and grace. Full of valves and transformers, the cameras were both heavy and hot – very different from the lightweight cameras and solid-state picture pickup devices of today.*

Right: *Colour television experiments had been conducted ever since John Logie Baird began in the late 1920s, but it was not until 1955 that the BBC started regular test transmissions (outside normal broadcasting hours). Early receivers were extremely large and cumbersome. Also, being hand-made prototypes, they were very expensive. The only opportunity the public had to see colour television during the 1950s was at special exhibitions.*

those days. Passing cars or a neighbour's vacuum cleaner caused patterns and lines that disrupted the picture. The BBC even showed an amusing public information film to alert inconsiderate motorists to the displeasure caused if they did not fit a suppressor.

Television affected even what people ate and the way they ate it. The first signs were innocent enough, when manufacturers started cashing in by selling 'television assortment' tins of biscuits and toffees, but then came the frozen 'TV dinner', designed to be eaten off a tray while watching programmes such as *Coronation Street* or the *Sixty-Four Thousand Dollar Question*. Commercials aimed at children implored 'Don't forget the fruit gums, Mum' or demonstrated the riot-quelling qualities of Nestlé's Milky Bar in the old Wild West. Adults were lured with the charms of Fry's Turkish Delight or were sold such obvious falsehoods as a chocolate bar that could be eaten between meals without ruining one's appetite. The era of what sociologists call the 'hidden persuaders' had arrived.

As the new interference suppression regulations make themselves felt, this is the question every customer will be asking. As time goes on, unsuppressed electrical appliances will become unsaleable. Make sure that the goods you manufacture or sell are effectively suppressed. In case of doubt, the Dubilier technical advisory service is at your command.

DUBILIER

Dubilier Condenser Co. (1925) Ltd., Ducon Works, Victoria Road, North Acton, London, W.3.   Telephone : ACOrn 2241
Grams : Hivoltcon Wesphone, London.   Marconi International Code

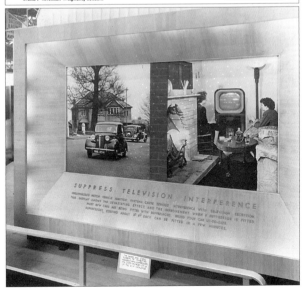

'Is it suppressed?' It is not a strange question that this housewife of 1956 is asking (above); unsuppressed appliances could ruin television viewing in those days, and so could cars. A graphic display by the Post Office (below) at the annual British Industries Fair demonstrates the interference that unsuppressed motor vehicles caused to television pictures and sound.

Left: *A mid 1950s advertisement for Rowntree's Fruit Gums. It had no caption or slogan but the message was clear enough. The television age was here.*

Below: *The invasion of television culture: television toffee tin, television money box, television cigarette lighter, even television egg cups.*

CHANNELS, STATIONS AND IDENTS

Terrestrial television programmes today reach us over a classification of airwaves called UHF or ultra-high frequencies. In the black and white era the programmes were broadcast on rather lower frequencies in the VHF (very high frequency) band, also known before the Second World War as the ultra-short wave or USW band.

Before the war there was just one television channel, unnumbered, as well as an auxiliary frequency used by the BBC for receiving outside broadcast contributions. After the war the BBC was allocated a total of five channels (1 to 5), designated as Band I. Band II is used for VHF FM radio broadcasting. Additional channels in Band III were provided for ITV (and also shared in a few locations by the BBC). These were numbered 6 to 14, although channel 14 was never used. The Republic of Ireland also had a 405-line television service, using some of these channels, and these Irish programmes could be received in parts of Wales and England. There were also plans for offshore 'pirate' television stations in the 1960s, but, unlike the radio ships, these never came to fruition.

As television expanded to cover the whole of Britain, additional transmitter stations were erected, often on windswept hills and crags with evocative names. Viewers who searched their atlases for magnificent titles such as Pontop Pike, North Hessary Tor, Holme Moss and Rumster Forest did so in vain, however, since the places they referred to were as obscure as the names mentioned in the shipping forecasts on the radio.

With the coming of independent television from 1955 onwards, there was a need to distinguish the separate stations and create a distinct on-screen character for each. Until then the BBC had not set out to create a strong visual identity, but with the advent of ITV everything changed. Each programme contractor now had its own brief jingle or musical 'calling card', as well as a more substantial piece of music played at the start of each day's transmissions. Many of these latter melodies were by composers of high standing; independent stations took themselves quite seriously.

Another brand-new feature was the animated visual 'ident': a spinning star for Associated-Rediffusion, the 'eyes' of ATV, and so on. The BBC commissioned an

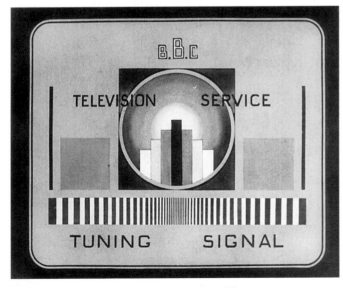

Test cards and other television graphics have attracted serious interest from design students and others. Echoes of Art Deco style can be seen in this pre-war BBC tuning signal used between programme transmissions.

23

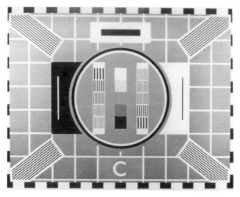

Left: *A recurring image of the 1950s was Test Card C, transmitted for long periods during the day to the accompaniment of light music. With no daytime programming to speak of, this was all that could be seen on both channels during the morning and afternoon. The various geometric patterns allowed engineers installing new television sets to adjust the picture for best focus and correct appearance, whilst the picture and music were also handy for in-store demonstrations.*

Right: *According to contemporary information, the BBC's 'Television Symbol' of the mid 1950s consisted of two intersecting eyes scanning the globe from north to south and from east to west, symbolising vision and the power of vision. Flashes of lightning on either side represented electrical forces, and the whole form took the shape of wings, suggesting the creative possibilities of television broadcasting. The BBC used this motif with gusto, not only on-screen but in publicity material, on canteen crockery and even as a sort of weathervane above the new Wood Lane Television Centre. The symbol's designer was Abram Games FSIA, a noted commercial artist who had also devised the symbol for the 1951 Festival of Britain.*

extremely intricate 'Television Symbol' that revolved in an almost impossible fashion between programmes, to the accompaniment of dainty but not very trendy 'Symbol Music' played on the celeste.

However, the BBC could not possibly match the commercials shown on ITV (to the great relief of many people). Viewers were treated (or subjected) to a remarkable or mind-numbing selection of advertisements, introduced by a variety of starburst animations unique to each station. These commercials owed a lot to contemporary American ideas, so a high proportion made use of cartoon animation and catchy jingles.

ABC Television Ltd. Midlands *Saturdays and Sundays* North of England *Saturdays and Sundays*	
Anglia Television Ltd. East Anglia *Whole week*	
Associated-Rediffusion Ltd. London *Mondays to Fridays*	
Associated TeleVision Ltd. London *Saturdays and Sundays* Midlands *Mondays to Fridays*	
Border Television Ltd. The Borders *Whole week*	
Channel Television Channel Islands *Whole week*	
Grampian Television Ltd. North-East Scotland *Whole week*	
Granada TV Network Ltd. North of England *Mondays to Fridays*	

	Scottish Television Ltd. Central Scotland *Whole week*
	Southern Television Ltd. Central Southern and South-East England *Whole week*
	T W W Ltd. South Wales and the West of England *Whole week*
	Tyne Tees Television North-East England *Whole week*
	Ulster Television Ltd. Northern Ireland *Whole week*
	Westward Television South-West England *Whole week*
	Independent Television News Ltd. Provides the main news bulletins for all Independent Television areas
	Independent Television Companies Association The Association acts on behalf of all the Programme Companies on certain matters of common interest

Right: *Some of these ITV companies from the mid 1960s still survive, but none of these logos is still in use.*

Left: *Working displays of old televisions, complete with their large V-shaped 'rabbit's ears' portable antennas, can be seen regularly at historical displays and collectors' swap-meets. The set on the right is a small-screen 'kitchen set' sold by Ferguson in the 1960s; it has separate tuning knobs for VHF (405-line) and UHF (625-line) programmes and was what might today be called 'future-proof'.*

Right: *Feel that cosy glow, experience the appeal of 'Sputnik' lights, TV tables and furniture in 'Contemporary' style! Those who enjoy re-creating room settings or whose inclination is towards a 'retro' lifestyle will find that an old television set can effectively complement period room decor.*

OLD TELEVISION TODAY

Attitudes towards television have changed greatly. Until the 1980s the subject was dismissed by many as an ephemeral and rather low-brow form of entertainment, whilst broadcasters generally felt uneasy about screening their heritage of old programmes for fear that more 'sophisticated' audiences might ridicule their older output. The coming of Channel Four, new satellite stations and the rise of home video have all created an insatiable demand for programme material, while a more enlightened attitude in the media has conditioned us to appreciate old television in a positive manner.

Pioneer groups such as Wider TV Access and Kaleidoscope proved there was a demand for viewing old programmes by arranging public screenings, whilst the opening of the Museum of the Moving Image in London and the National Museum of Photography, Film and Television in Bradford have also made an interest in old television respectable. Today there is no shortage of books, societies and conventions devoted to old television. Archive recordings are screened on television and can be bought on videotape, whilst the BBC and the National Film and Television Archive have had success in tracking down 'lost' programmes and returning them to the archive. 'Kaleidoscope' and 'Missing, Believed Wiped' are the titles of annual conventions devoted to old television in general, whilst specialist groups hold their own events related to *Doctor Who* and other tele-fantasy programmes.

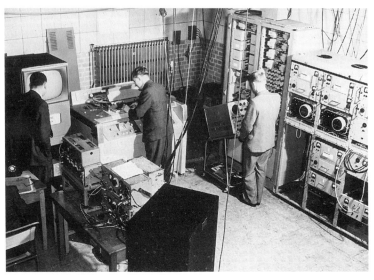

A constant regret is how few television programmes were recorded in the past. One of the reasons for this is the sheer size and expense of the equipment needed to make recordings in those days. Here an Ampex 1000 machine is being put through its paces in the BBC research laboratories. These huge machines, which were the state of the art around 1960, used tape 2 inches (5 cm) wide and were certainly not suitable for use in one's living room!

COLLECTING AND RESTORING OLD TV SETS

This is an absorbing and not necessarily expensive hobby. For technical and safety reasons, electrical restoration should be handled only by qualified people. Even though there are no longer any transmissions on the 405-line standard, converters can be had to adapt these old sets to modern programmes and video recorders. For a fact sheet send a stamped addressed envelope to: Factsheet, 71 Falcutt Way, Northampton NN2 8PH.

TELEVISION MUSIC

There is a strong interest in old theme tunes, production and presentation music, whilst even test-card music has a keen following of its own. In the 1960s, for instance, ITV played popular and classical music from commercial albums, whilst the BBC played light music that was recorded specially for test-card performance. Because the BBC's music was not for sale in the shops, a cult following grew, and CD albums of original test-

When the BBC launched electronic television in 1936, programmes were provided initially using Marconi-EMI or Baird equipment in alternate weeks. The latter employed film taken by a cine camera, which was processed, developed and scanned electronically in less than a minute after shooting. This is the actual camera used in that near-instantaneous 'Intermediate Film' process; it was discovered in a cine enthusiast's garage and is now in the National Museum of Photography, Film and Television at Bradford.

This unassuming looking wooden construction found in a car boot sale in Dublin was recognised as the hulk of a mechanical television receiver of the early 1930s. Despite its scruffy appearance, it is a unique and valuable relic of the earliest days of television; similar treasures can still be found by those with eyes to see them.

card music have been released. Specialist groups (see 'Societies and Information Sources') exist to channel the interest in television music and allied matters such as the films shown for trade test transmission purposes in the early days of colour television in Britain.

TELEVISION ARCHAEOLOGY

So poorly was the early history of television preserved that museums and archives are relying on the public to rediscover lost treasures. Programmes on film, thought to have been lost forever, have been rediscovered, often by enthusiasts searching through attics and junk shops. Regular screenings of these and other old television programmes are held at the National Film Theatre in London under the title 'Missing, Believed Wiped' (see 'Places to Visit'). The so-called Intermediate Film Process camera used by Baird in 1935-6 was found in a cine collector's garage, and fortunately this unique artefact was recognised by another collector and saved for the nation. Other rare items have turned up in house clearances.

Collecting television knick-knacks from the 1950s and 1960s can be a very enjoyable hobby. This display in a museum that is now closed shows a ship's wheel lamp for giving dim illumination while viewing television, money boxes, filmstrip viewers, other toys, an aerial 'booster' and a converter for adapting a BBC-only television to receive ITV programmes in addition.

At the Amberley Museum in West Sussex a replica television dealer's showroom has been built and houses a superb display of old televisions and video recorders.

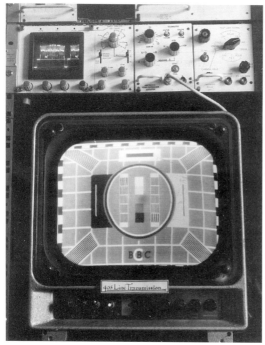

Britain's pioneer 405-line television system may be technically obsolete, but the nostalgic appeal of the old technology will live on for many years to come. Museums and enthusiastic collectors will both work together to ensure this, as seen in this display at the Vintage Wireless Museum in London.

IMPORTANT DATES IN TELEVISION HISTORY

1925 John Logie Baird makes the world's first public demonstration of television in Selfridge's department store, London.

1926 Television Ltd (later known as Baird Television) receives the first licence in the world issued specifically for the transmission of television pictures.

1928 The world's first transatlantic television transmission of live pictures from amateur radio station G2KZ at Coulsdon, Surrey, received in New York.

1929 Baird begins thirty-line transmissions over BBC airwaves (ended 1935).

1936 The BBC opens the first public electronic television system in the world.

1937 Electronic television starts in France, from the Eiffel Tower transmitter on 455 lines.

1938 Electronic television starts in Germany (Berlin, 441 lines).

1939 RCA introduces electronic television in the USA, at the New York World's Fair (441 lines). Afterwards the outbreak of war puts an end to television broadcasting in Britain and most other countries.

1946 Television reopens in London.

1949 First provincial transmitter in Britain (Sutton Coldfield, serving the Midlands).

1950 First television outside broadcast from the continent (Calais *en Fête*).

1951 Bing Crosby Enterprises in California demonstrate the first professional video recorder, using tape moving at 100 inches (254 cm) per second.

1953 Coronation ceremony televised in Britain and relayed to western Europe by Eurovision.

1954 First full Eurovision link-up; eight countries take part.

1955 BBC commences experimental colour transmissions (405 lines, American NTSC colour process). Commercial television (ITV) opens in Britain, but in the London area only.

1956 ITV extended to the Midlands and North regions.

1957 ITV opens in Scotland. The 'toddlers' truce' (an hour-long gap in programming between 6 and 7 pm to allow mothers to put children to bed) ends.

1958 ITV reaches South Wales, the West and Southern England.

1959 ITV is extended to North-east England, Northern Ireland and the East of England. Toshiba in Japan introduces the helical scan system of videotape recording, the tape running at 15 inches (38 cm) per second.

1960 ITV opens in South-east England.

1961 ITV expands into South-west England, North-east Scotland and the Borders.

1962 British viewers see the first live pictures from the USA, via the Telstar satellite. ITV moves into North and West Wales and the Channel Isles, becoming available to 96 per cent of the population.

1964 BBC2 opens on 625 lines.

1965 Cigarette commercials banned on ITV.

1968 Major reorganisation of ITV franchises brings in Thames, Yorkshire, Harlech and London Weekend Television.

1969 Colour television introduced by ITV and BBC1. Sony Corporation produce their colour cassette video recorder.

With the opening of television in 1936 the BBC broke new ground in more ways than one. What were the legal and copyright positions? Nobody was quite sure, so the BBC decided to take no chances by showing this caption.

FURTHER READING

Bennett-Levy, Michael. *Historic Televisions and Video Recorders.* MBL Publications (Monkton House, Old Craighall, Musselburgh, Midlothian EH21 8SF), 1993. Large colour illustrated paperback.

Bennett-Levy, Michael. *Tv Is King.* MBL Publications, 1994. Sequel to the above title, with more sumptuous colour illustrations.

Cornell, Paul; Day, Martin; and Topping, Keith. *Classic British TV.* Guinness Books, 1993. Substantial in-depth study of over one hundred classic and well-loved programmes.

Kingsley, Hilary, and Tibballs, Geoff. *Box of Delights.* Macmillan, 1989. Covers the period from the 1950s to the 1980s. Programmes, personalities and even favourite commercials are all included, plus a 'Where are they now?' section. Thoroughly researched and well written.

Lazell, David. *What's on the Box?* Evergreen (PO Box 52, Cheltenham GL50 1YQ), 1991. An engaging history of television viewing from early times to modern.

Tibballs, Geoff. *Golden Age of Children's Television.* Titan Books, 1991. Large format paperback covering the years 1950 to 1975.

Vahimagi, Tise. *British Television.* Oxford University Press, 1994. Large illustrated paperback with detailed entries on more than 1100 favourite television programmes from 1936 to the present.

SOCIETIES AND SOURCES OF INFORMATION

When writing to these societies please send a stamped addressed envelope with all enquiries.

Alexandra Palace Television Society: Simon Vaughan, Archivist APTS, 30 Firsgrove Crescent, Brentwood, Essex CM14 5JL. The society is compiling an archive of photographs, drawings, reminiscences and film concerning the Alexandra Palace studios and transmitters.

Alexandra Palace Television Trust: Alexandra Palace, Wood Green, London N22 4AY. The trust aims to open a museum of television history at the Palace.

British Vintage Wireless Society: Gerald Wells, Vintage Wireless Museum, 23 Rosendale Road, London SE21 8DS. Many television collectors belong to BVWS, which often has articles on vintage television in its magazine.

Narrow Bandwidth TV Association: 1 Burnwood Drive, Wollaton, Nottingham NG8 2DJ. The NBTVA newsletter covers Baird-era topics.

Robert Farnon Society: Stone Gables, Upton Lane, Seavington St Michael, Ilminster, Somerset TA19 0PZ. Covers light music in all its forms, including television signature themes, production music and the like.

STARS (Savers of Television And Radio Shows): care of Malcolm Chapman, 96 Meadvale Road, London W5 1NR. Members lend each other copies of old programmes.

Test Card Circle: 2 Henderson Row, Edinburgh EH3 5DS. Publishes a regular magazine full of articles on test-card music and trade test films.

Test Card Club: 7 Epping Close, Derby DE3 4HR. Quarterly magazine on test-card related topics.

405 Alive: Larkhill, Newport Road, Woodseaves, Stafford ST20 0NP. The only magazine in the world devoted to the vintage television hobby in all its forms.

PLACES TO VISIT

Before travelling, intending visitors are advised to find out the times of opening and to check that particular items of interest will be on display.

Amberley Museum, Houghton Bridge, Amberley, Arundel, West Sussex BN18 9LT. Telephone: 01798 831370. Comprehensive industrial archaeology museum, with a superb selection of old television sets in a reconstructed radio and television showroom of the 1950s (further information from Ron Weller on 01903 267839).

Design Museum, Butler's Wharf, Shad Thames, London SE1 2YD. Telephone: 0171-403 6933. A small number of design-classic sets are on show.

Museum of the Moving Image (MOMI), South Bank, Waterloo, London SE1 8XT. Telephone: 0171-928 3535 (switchboard) or 0171-401 2636 (recorded information line). Exhibits include old television cameras, 1950s living room with period set playing old programmes.

National Museum of Photography, Film and Television, Pictureville, Bradford, West Yorkshire BD1 1NQ. Telephone: 01274 727488. Good displays of old television cameras and receivers. The 'TV Heaven' exhibit allows visitors to enter a 'time capsule' and recapture the impression of television viewing in the past. (Closed for redevelopment until 1999.)

National Vintage Wireless and Television Museum, The High Lighthouse, West Street, Harwich, Essex CO7 6HG. Telephone: 01206 322606.

'On the Air' Broadcasting Museum, 42 Bridge Street Row, Chester CH1 1NN. Telephone: 01244 348468. Small but comprehensive museum and shop combined.

Vintage Wireless Museum, 23 Rosendale Road, West Dulwich, London SE21 8DS. Telephone: 0181-670 3667. Delightful museum with working pre-war television sets and ex-BBC standard converters. Not always open; visitors must telephone first for an appointment.

York Castle Museum, Eye of York, York YO1 1RY. Telephone: 01904 653611. Exhibits include a 1950s living room and a Bush TV22 set on which one can watch *Hancock's Half Hour.* The 'Every Home Should Have One' gallery includes different types of set, with excerpts from a 1950s programme.

There are also plans for a museum of television at the historic Alexandra Palace site in north London.

COLLECTORS' FAIRS

Bakelite Fair: held at the De La Warr Pavilion, Bexhill, East Sussex, in May. Organised by the Bakelite Museum Society (telephone: 0181-852 3492 or 0374 126670).

Memorabilia Roadshow and Fairs: held at the National Exhibition Centre, Birmingham; City Halls, Glasgow; Bowler's, Trafford Park, Manchester. Contact: Made in Heaven, 216 Kristiansand Way, Letchworth, Hertfordshire SG6 1TU (telephone: 01462 683965 or 0860 355620).

National Vintage Communications Fair: held at the National Exhibition Centre, Birmingham, in May and October. Organised by Jonathan Hill, 13 Belmont Road, Exeter, Devon EX1 2HF (telephone/fax: 01392 411565).

SCREENINGS OF OLD PROGRAMMES

Kaleidoscope. Kaleidoscope has been organising acclaimed screenings of classic British television since 1988. All proceeds go to charity. A wide range of programmes is shown at events held periodically in Stourbridge Town Hall, West Midlands. For further information send a stamped addressed envelope to Kaleidoscope, 93 Old Park Road, Dudley, West Midlands DY1 3NE.

National Film Theatre, South Bank, London SE1 8TL (telephone: 0171-815 1374). Regular seasons of old television programmes, plus discussions and debates. 'Missing, Believed Wiped', the special annual presentation of lost classics rediscovered, has become an institution.